What Do Machines Do All Day?

by Jo Nelson

Illustrated by Aleksandar Savić

WIDE EYED EDITIONS

Contents

Are you ready for an adventure?

Come with us and find out what machines do...

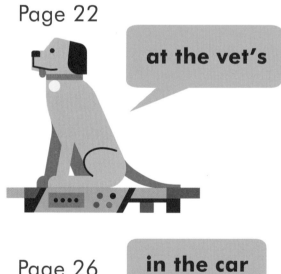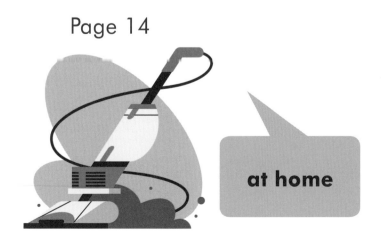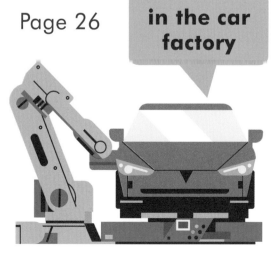

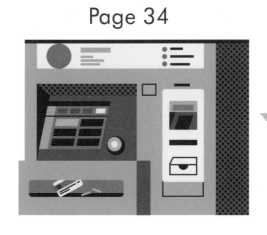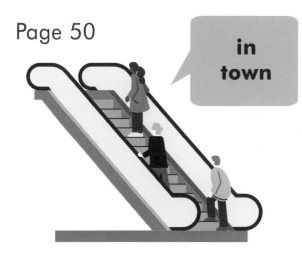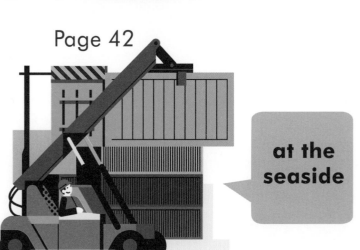

What do machines do all day?

On this trip, we are going to tour 14 different places. After visiting each place, you can learn about eight special machines that work there.

Then you can go back and try to spot each of the machines in action. Can you spot them all?

There are machines all around us. They can be small enough to hold, as big as a person or bigger than a car. They've been invented and created to make our lives easier...

But what do they do all day?

They move and make noises and do special jobs. Some machines need people to hold them, push them, or ride in them. Others are programmed to work automatically. Each machine is carefully designed to suit its job and location. It may have chunky wheels, robot arms, flashing lights, even whirring blades.

Join us on our adventure as we visit some very different places. Whether you're on a muddy farm, at a super-clean vet's office, down a dusty mine, or on a busy film set, you'll be amazed by the range of machines at work.

Welcome to the farm

Machines are always chugging and humming away on a farm. They plow the fields, sow the seeds, and harvest the crops. Meanwhile, the cows need to be milked, the sheep must be sheared, and the grass needs cutting. It's going to be a busy day!

What do machines do on the farm?

I cut and collect the ripe golden wheat, then separate the wheat grains from their stalks.

I can pull trailers, mowers, and plows. My chunky wheels are good for driving on uneven ground.

My thick blades churn and break up the rich, bare soil. I prepare the fields for seeds to be sown.

I sow tiny seeds in neat rows in the soil. They whiz down my pipes and pop out onto the soil.

A tractor pulls me over the emerald-green fields. My sharp blades mow down the long, lush grass.

I collect up the grass and shape it into bales. The grass dries into hay for animals to munch on in winter.

The farmer attaches me to the cow's udders. Milk comes rushing through my tubes and collects in a container.

I shear off the sheep's hot, fluffy fleeces. The old fleeces are taken away to be turned into wool.

Welcome to the building site

Through the dust and dirt, machines both large and small dig, drill, lift, and carry. They are turning a patch of mud and rubble into some new homes for people to live in.

What do machines do on a building site?

I dig out soil using a large bucket on my long hydraulic arm. I carry it to the dump truck and dump it in.

I pick up heavy loads of rock and soil and move them around. When I lift up my back, everything slides out.

I churn concrete in my truck and pump it along a pipe to where it's needed on the building site.

I lift large, heavy objects into place on the new building. My long tower means I can lift things up very high.

I roll along on my wide caterpillar tracks. My giant front shovel smooths and flattens the ground.

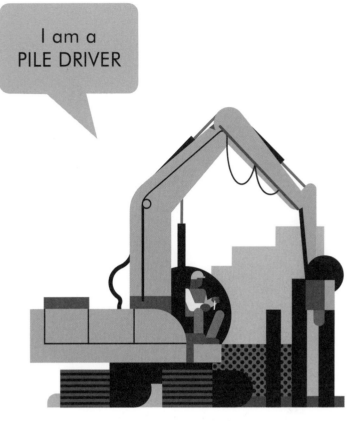

I drive strong poles called piles deep into the ground. The piles will give the new building support.

My sides open up like scissors and lift my platform up. I carry builders to different parts of the building.

I beat down on the surface below me to make it flat and firm before it becomes the floor for a new room.

Welcome to our home

Our lives are made much easier, warmer, and tidier by the machines in and around our homes. Have you ever stopped to think about the jobs they do?

What do machines do in the house?

I am a BOILER

I heat water and send it to the faucet and showers, as well as the radiators.

I am a WASHING MACHINE

I soak, swish, drain, and spin your clothes to wash away the dirt.

I am a TUMBLE DRYER

I dry your clothes by spinning them in hot air, which removes the moisture until they are dry.

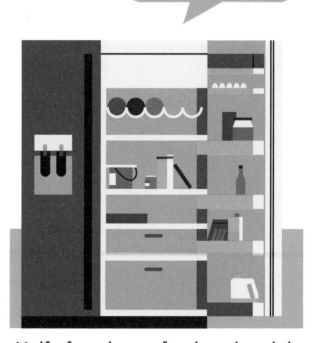

I am a REFRIGERATOR

Half of me keeps food cool and the other half freezes it. When food is cool, it is harder for bacteria to grow.

I am a
TOILET

I collect pee and poop. When you flush me, water carries the waste away through pipes to the sewer.

I am a
VACUUM
CLEANER

I suck up dust, dirt, and crumbs from the floor. I have special attachments for carpets and awkward corners.

I am a
WEED
WHACKER

I have a strong, long plastic wire inside me. I spin the end around very quickly to cut down weeds and long grass.

I am a
LAWN MOWER

Push me around your lawn and my spinning blades will cut the grass as I go. I collect the cut grass in a bag.

Welcome to the office

Office workers rely on electronic machines, especially computers, to speed up the jobs they do. Meanwhile, other machines help office life run smoothly.

What do machines do in the office?

When you push my button, my doors will close and a motor above me will move me up or down to the floor you need.

I shred unwanted, important papers into thin strips so that no one can read them. This keeps business information private.

I record, store, and process information. I can connect to the printer, the internet, and other networks.

I can print, scan, and photocopy documents. I keep printing ink and two types of paper inside me.

I make coffee by grinding up coffee beans, pressing them, and passing hot water through them.

I keep water in me and cool it down, ready for people to have a refreshing drink.

I keep the office cool. I use a coolant to take the heat out of the air. My fan moves the air around.

I blast narrow strips of air at your hands, which will blow off the water and dry them quickly.

Welcome to the vet's

People bring their animals here for check-ups or when they're sick. Vets use lots of clever machines. Some machines figure out what's happening inside the animal. Others help make the animal better.

What do machines do at the vet's?

When an animal stands on me, I tell the vet how much it weighs. This helps the vet to know how healthy the animal is.

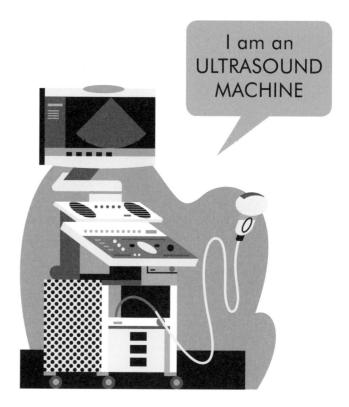

I send pulses of sound into the animal's body. I use the echoes to create a picture of what's inside.

I use special gases to keep animals numb, comfortable, and asleep when they are having operations.

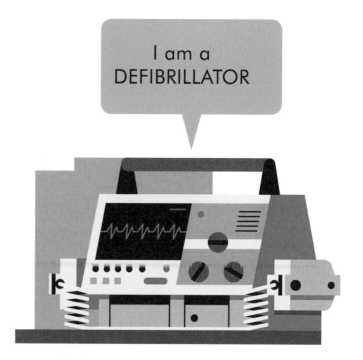

If an animal's heart stops working properly, I can give it an electric shock and get it beating normally again.

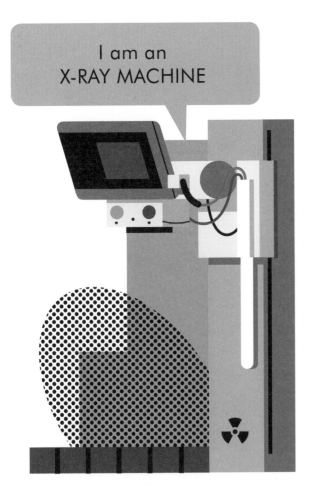

I am an
X-RAY MACHINE

I take pictures of animals' skeletons using X-rays. The vet can then spot if a bone is broken.

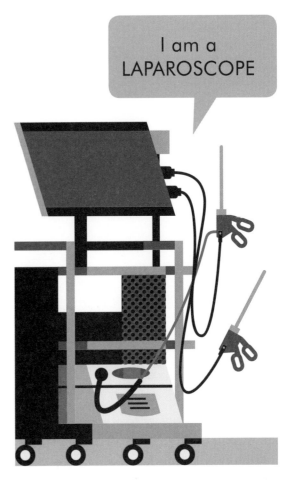

I am a
LAPAROSCOPE

I'm a tube with a camera on it that goes inside the body. I show vets what's going on and help them do operations.

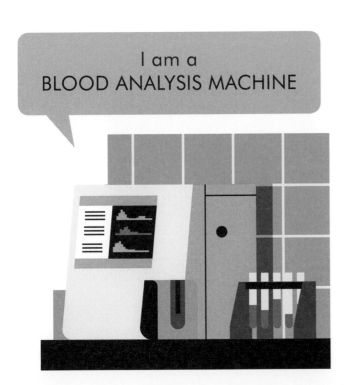

I am a
BLOOD ANALYSIS MACHINE

Blood is made up of red and white blood cells and platelets. I count how many there are of each to help the vet figure out what's wrong.

I am a
MICROSCOPE

My lenses make tiny objects look much bigger. Vets use me to look for unusual things they can't see with the naked eye.

Welcome to the car factory

It's a whirl of high-tech machinery in here. Machines on wheels and rails move car parts from one place to the next, while robots perform precise jobs along the assembly line.

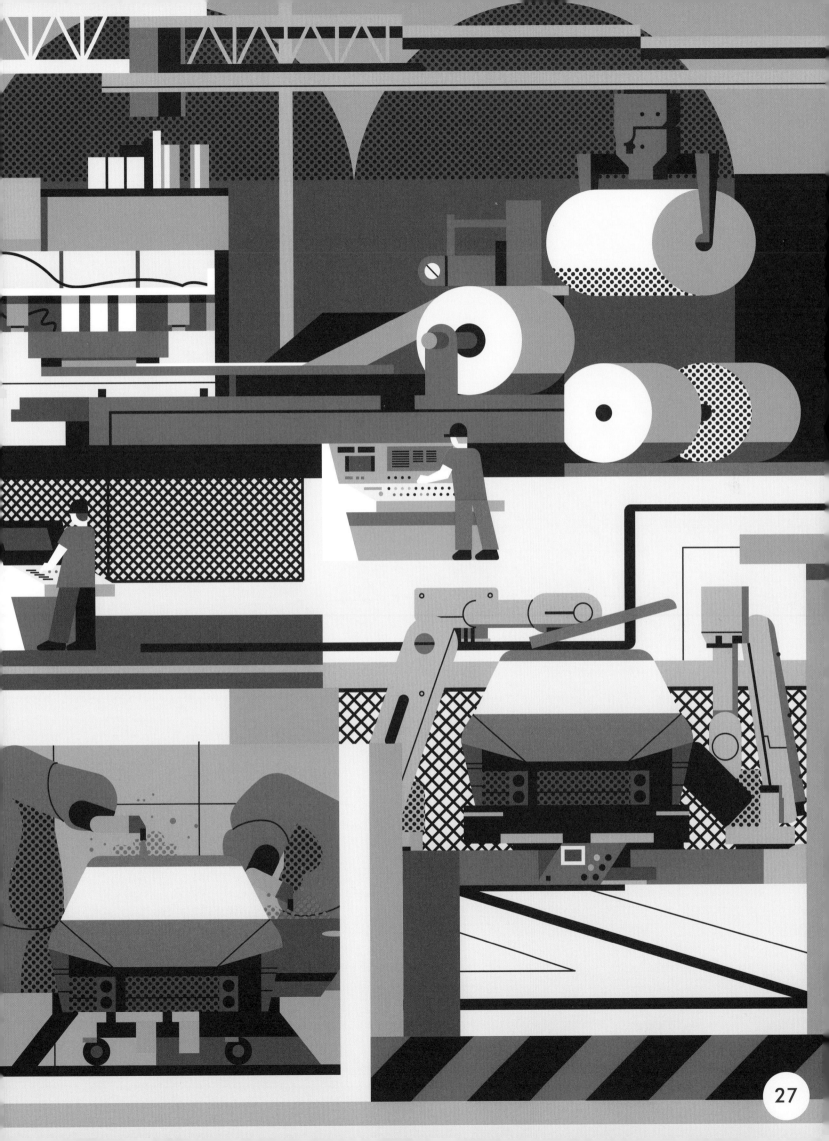

What do machines do in a car factory?

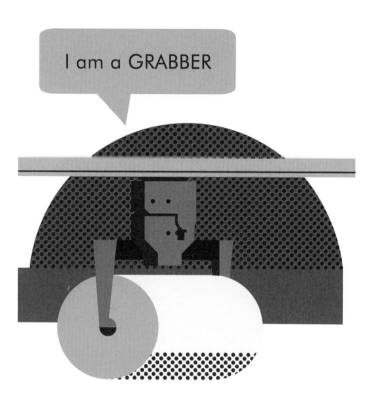

I am a GRABBER

I move along attached to rails on the ceiling. My big metal jaws pick up and move rolls of thin, metal aluminium sheets.

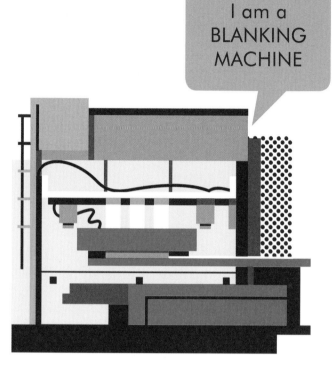

I am a BLANKING MACHINE

I unroll the aluminium sheet, feed it inside me, then chop it into more useful-sized rectangles.

I am an AUTOMATED GUIDED VEHICLE

I don't need a driver. I follow magnetic lines on the floor to move car parts around the assembly line.

I am a WELDING ROBOT

I use heat to melt metal and stick different car parts together. This way of sticking metal is called welding.

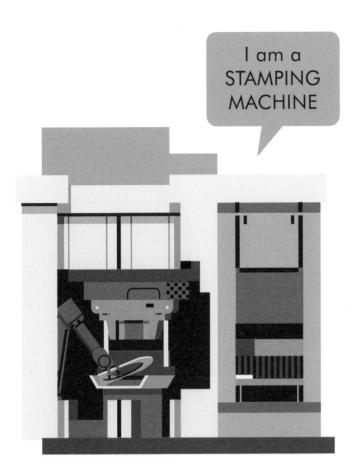

I squash the aluminium rectangles into different shapes to make car parts, from doors to hoods.

I carry car parts around the factory. I place my metal prongs under them, lift them up, and carry them off.

I spray the car shell with an even layer of shiny, colored paint. I wear a special jacket to protect me from the paint.

My arms can move in all directions. I pick up car seats or windows and carefully fit them into the car.

Welcome to the film set

Lights, camera, action! It's busy on the film set as machines help the film crew to get the best angles, sounds, and footage for their next blockbuster movie.

What do machines do on a film set?

I am a LIGHTING CRANE

I stretch my long neck to raise the powerful lighting rig up and above the film set. Then it can cast light on the action below.

I am a CAMERA

I capture the moving images in front of me through my wide lens.

I am a CAMERA DOLLY

I carry the camera along a little railway. I make sure that the camera stays steady as it moves around.

I am a MICROPHONE

I listen to sounds and send them to the mixing desk. I'm fixed on the end of a pole called a boom.

I receive sounds from the microphone. I adjust the sound levels so one noise doesn't drown out the others.

I'm a moving arm fixed to a tripod on wheels. I carry the camera and hold it in the right position.

If a film set isn't near a main electricity supply, I make electricity for the machines.

I appear at the beginning of every shot with the date and time written on me. When I snap shut, the action begins.

Welcome to the train station

From buying a ticket or a snack to checking your train time and getting through the turnstile, there are all kinds of machines you can use at a station.

What do machines do at the train station?

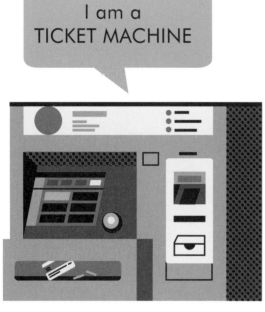

I am a TICKET MACHINE

I am a computer and a printer. Choose where you want to go, give me some money, and I will print you a ticket.

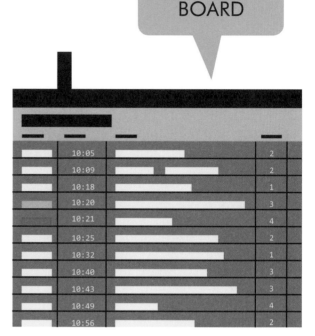

I am a DEPARTURES BOARD

I show up-to-date information about what time the trains will leave the station and from which platform.

I am an ELECTRIC CART

I carry people and luggage up and down the platform. My electric engine is very quiet.

I am a LOCOMOTIVE

I'm the powerful train engine that drives the carriages. I run on diesel fuel. My wheels follow the railway line.

Insert your ticket in my slot or scan your ticket code on my glass panel and I will let you through.

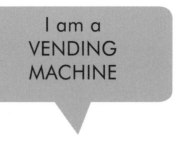

Feeling hungry? Choose a snack, put your money in the slot, and I'll drop the food in the drawer for you to eat.

I push gravel beneath the rail track. This makes the base stronger and keeps the metal rails level.

I grind away any rusty or bumpy parts on the rails so the train can glide easily along the tracks.

SPEED
LIMIT
30

YOUR SPEED

Welcome to the open road

Cars and trucks zoom around every day, but can you spot and name the other machines that mend our roads and keep the traffic flowing?

What do machines do on the road?

I lay down new road surfaces. I churn out asphalt as a hot, flat strip that sticks to the ground, cools, and sets hard.

I carry the ingredients for a new road surface—a sticky, dark, crumbly mixture called asphalt.

I show drivers warnings about the stretch of road coming up. This one means there are two lanes closed ahead.

I watch cars driving along the road and flash up a warning sign if they are going at a dangerous speed.

I ride over the newly laid road, pressing it down as I go. I have two heavy rollers instead of wheels.

My radar detects the speed of vehicles going by. If they're speeding, I take a picture and tell the traffic police.

When my red light is on, I'm saying "stop and wait to cross the road." My green light means "it's safe to cross."

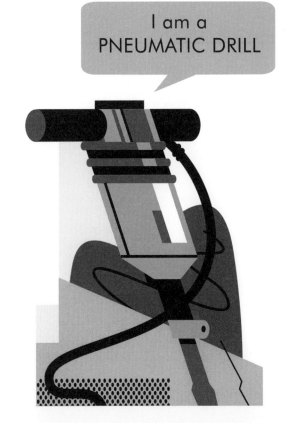

Workmen use me to make holes in the road. "Pneumatic" means I'm powered by air that's squashed under pressure.

41

Welcome to the seaside

See the machines at work in the busy port, loading and unloading heavy containers from the ships. Take a short stroll along the beach and you'll notice more helpful machines in action.

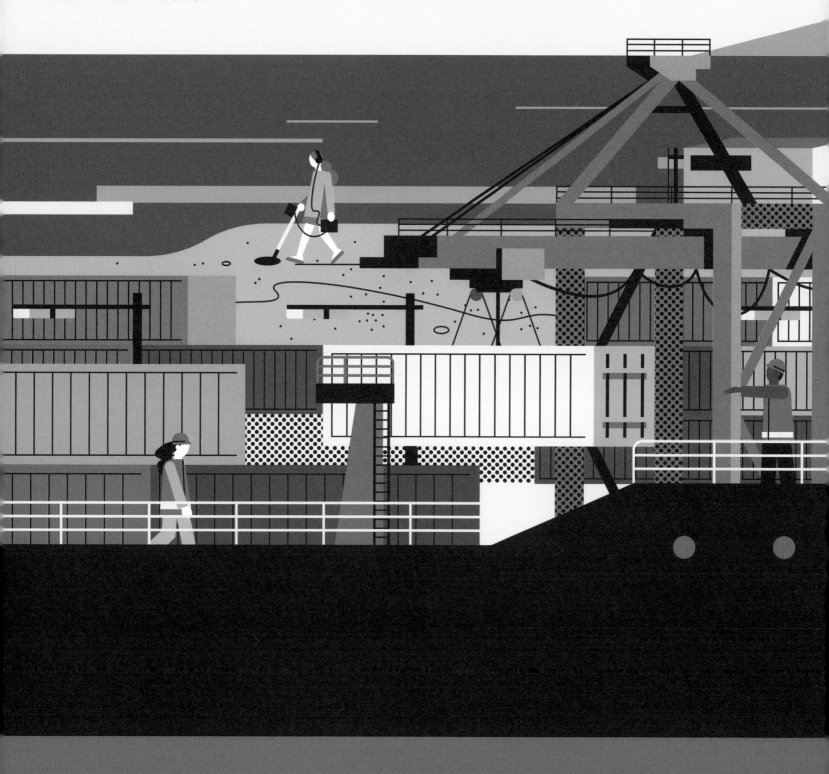

What do machines do at the seaside?

I am an ANCHOR WINDLASS

I raise and lower the big anchor at the front of the ship. I roll up and unroll the anchor chain using my motor.

I am a REACH STACKER

I unload colorful metal containers from trucks and stack them on the dockyard. Then I load them onto ships.

I am a LIGHTHOUSE

I stand on the headland and warn ships about dangerous rocks around me by flashing my electric light.

I am a LIFEBOAT LAUNCHER

I carry a lifeboat down the beach and reverse into the shallow water. The lifeboat then launches off into the sea.

I put containers on ships and take them off. I use a spreader that clips on to the top of the container to help me hold on to it.

I carry metal containers to and from ships. They fit securely on my long, flat back.

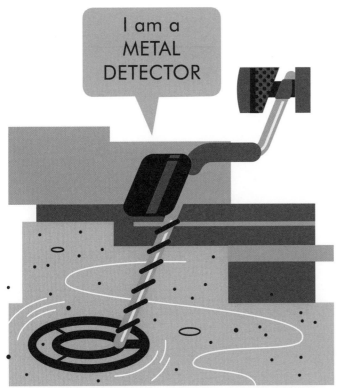

Sweep me along the beach and I'll beep when I detect something metal in the sand below.

I am pushed along the beach like a lawn mower. I smooth down the sand and scoop up any litter left behind.

Welcome to the restaurant kitchen

With many hungry people to feed, there's lots of food that needs preparing and cooking—and plates that need washing. Luckily for the chefs, they have special machines to help them save time.

What do machines do in the kitchen?

I am a MIXER

I have different attachments for whisking, kneading, or mixing the ingredients in my bowl.

I am a WEIGHING SCALE

When you place an item on my flat surface, I show you the exact weight on my digital display.

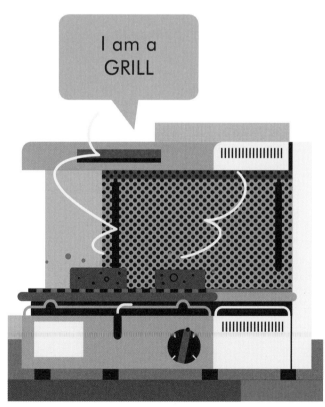

I am a GRILL

I have thin metal bars under my hood that heat up and cook food placed underneath.

I am an OVEN

I heat up the air inside me and move it around with a fan. Put food inside me to roast but don't forget to wear oven mitts!

I am a **POTATO PEELER**

I rumble potatoes and water around inside me. As they bash against my rough sides, their peel comes off.

I am a **POTATO CHIPPER**

I spin potatoes around inside me, pushing them through my sharp blades so they come out chip-shaped.

I am a **VENT**

It can get steamy and smoky in a kitchen. I use a fan to suck in the kitchen smells and send them outside.

I am a **DISHWASHER**

I wash trays of dirty crockery, blasting off the leftover food and leaving it sparkling clean.

Welcome to the town

There is more happening on the streets of town than meets the eye. From inside shops to at the park, machines are busy at work. They keep our town clean and help things run smoothly.

What do machines do in town?

There's no need to push me open or pull me closed. I sense your arrival and start to rotate so you can walk inside the building.

I'm a moving staircase. When a stair reaches the top, it disappears from view and reappears at the bottom again.

Put in your bank card and tell me how much money you want. I will talk to your bank and give you money from your account.

I drive along the street and sweep with my circular brushes. They loosen litter for me to then suck up like a vacuum cleaner.

Show me the barcodes on your items and place them in my bagging area. Then put money in the slot to pay.

I'm a calculator and a money box. The cashier pushes my buttons to figure out the price, then puts money in my drawer.

I drive to your street and eat what's inside your recycling bin. When I'm full, I go to the recycling center and empty myself.

I blow leaves off paths and lawns and put them into big piles. My motor and fan fit in a handy backpack.

Welcome to the mine

Deep underground, machines are churning through rock and cutting out useful materials to bring to the surface. It's a complicated job that needs careful planning and specialized equipment.

What do machines do in a mine?

I spin my blades to push air through the mine shafts and tunnels. This means the workers have fresh air to breathe.

I'm shorter than other dump trucks so that I can fit through the mine's tunnels. I carry heavy loads up to the surface.

I break medium-sized rocks into small ones by crushing them in my tough metal jaws.

I carry small stones through the tunnels on my long wide belt. The stone can then be collected by trucks.

I have a pneumatic arm that hits rock with great force. I do this to smash big rocks into smaller ones.

I'm short and strong like the dump truck. I have a huge scoop at the front to load the truck with.

I use strong metal cables to pull up rock and useful materials in large metal cages.

There's lots of water underground. I pump it up and out so that the tunnels don't flood.

Welcome to the theme park

It takes some amazing machines to make a theme park thrilling. After spinning and turning and bumping and rolling, you'll be in need of a snack and some calming music!

What do machines do at a theme park?

I drag my carriages to the top of the first railway slope...then let go. Watch them whiz up, down, and around the track.

I'm a giant wheel with seats in pods at the end of my long spokes. I turn slowly so you can enjoy the view.

I spin around. I have painted wooden horses for passengers to ride on. As I turn, the horses move up and down.

I spin, getting faster until my passengers are pushed against my sides and they no longer need a floor to stand on!

I zoom around a mini lake. My motor turns my propellers, which moves me forward through the water.

I am a tiny car. Brushes underneath me make contact with the metal floor to give me the electricity I need to move.

I make a sweet fluffy treat out of colored sugar. I spin around and make tiny strands of melted sugar.

I pipe music around the theme park. The music is written down as a stamped-out code, which I turn into sound.

Index of machines

milking machine	9	shredder	20
mine dump truck	56	speed camera	41
mixer	48	speed limit sign	40
mixer pump truck	12	stamping machine	29
mixing desk	33	street sweeper	52
mower	9	tamper	37
oven	48	ticket machine	36
paint-spraying robot	29	tilt-a-whirl	60
paver	40	tip-up truck	40
pile driver	13	toilet	17
plate compactor	13	tractor	8
plow	8	traffic light	41
pneumatic drill	41	tumble dryer	16
potato chipper	49	turnstile	37
potato peeler	49	ultrasound machine	24
printer	20	vacuum cleaner	17
pump	57	vending machine	37
reach stacker	44	vent	49
recycling truck	53	ventilation fan	56
refrigerator	16	warning sign	40
revolving door	52	washing machine	16
rock breaker	57	water cooler	21
roller	41	weed whacker	17
roller coaster	60	weighing scale	24
scissor lift	13	weighing scale	48
seed drill	8	welding robot	28
self-checkout	53	winding tower	57
sheep shearer	9	X-ray machine	25

Inspiring | Educating | Creating | Entertaining

Brimming with creative inspiration, how-to projects, and useful information to enrich your everyday life, Quarto Knows is a favorite destination for those pursuing their interests and passions. Visit our site and dig deeper with our books into your area of interest: Quarto Creates, Quarto Cooks, Quarto Homes, Quarto Lives, Quarto Drives, Quarto Explores, Quarto Gifts, or Quarto Kids.

First published in 2019 by Wide Eyed Editions, an imprint of The Quarto Group.
400 First Avenue North, Suite 400, Minneapolis, MN 55401, USA.
T (612) 344-8100 F (612) 344-8692 **www.QuartoKnows.com**

ISBN 978-1-78603-466-3

The illustrations were created digitally
Set in Futura

Published by Jenny Broom and Rachel Williams
Designed by Karissa Santos
Edited by Lucy Brownridge
Production by Jenny Cundill

Manufactured in Dongguan, China TL 122018

9 8 7 6 5 4 3 2 1